How to NAVIGATE BEING SINGLE —

and savor your dating adventure

— A Life Guide —

How to NAVIGATE BEING SINGLE —

and savor your dating adventure

— A Life Guide —

Created by

DR. SUZANNE GELB, PhD, JD

FIRST EDITION

All rights reserved. This book or any portion thereof may not be reproduced or used in any manner whatsoever without the express written permission of the publisher except for the use of brief quotations in a book review.

Copyright © 2019 Dr. Suzanne J. Gelb, Ph.D., J.D.

Manufactured in the United States of America.

ISBN-13: 978-1-950764-09-9
ISBN-10: 1-950764-09-5

www.DrSuzanneGelb.com

PRAISE FOR... THE LIFE GUIDES

I wrote this life guide on handling the challenges of being single and enjoying the dating adventure, as well as 10 other life guides on various topics, to help readers successfully navigate some of life's trickiest challenges.

Each Life Guide includes educational information sourced from my three+ decades of coaching and counseling in the field of emotional wellness.

What Readers Are Saying

"Let's be honest: there's a lot of crappy dating advice out there. But Dr. Gelb's Life Guide is a cut above the rest.

This is sincere, heart-centered, healthy wisdom that WILL help singles find their special someone."

—Annika Martins

"Dr. Gelb has a gentle spirit that instantly makes you feel like you've come home. The depth of her wisdom is undeniable, her curiosity is insatiable and her love is palpable. These qualities make her the perfect guide for life.

In the pages of the Life Guides you will find practical and proven processes to support you in living your great life.

Whether it's heart-centered wisdom on navigating the dating world, love-based strategies for becoming a parent, or reaching your ideal weight through kindness, Dr. Gelb's Life Guides are gifts to be treasured."

—Dr. Gemma Stone, psychologist

"Dr. Gelb is a voice for real people in real life situations looking for help.

Her guide for singles takes you through both the emotional preparation for getting yourself out there, as well as specific steps to tackle online dating, pre-date prep and rejection.

In an easily digestible size, with clear language, this guide is the perfect companion for the single girl (or guy). Thank you Suzanne!"

—Pascale Kavanagh

"Inspiring, very informative, and so helpful.

The writing exercises in particular, are valuable for getting in touch with feelings and desires.

Partner with this Guide to find your one-in-a-lifetime partner! I recommend this Guide to clients and to all my single friends!"

—Alicia L

"Learning how to love yourself and treat yourself kindly — even when your life, career, body, and relationships aren't 'totally perfect' — is one of the hardest things to do.

Dr. Suzanne Gelb breaks down the art of self-love into practical steps. No woo-woo vagueness. Just easy-to-follow exercises pulled from her 28-year career in the field.

If you're looking for practicality and effectiveness, these Life Guides are a steal of a deal."

—Susan Hyatt, Master Certified Life Coach, Published Author

"Your guidebooks are gems."

—Alexandra Franzen, Published Author, Writing Teacher

CONTENTS

Disclaimer   xv

INTRODUCTION

With the Right Mindset and Practices, Finding True Love Can Be Truly Delightful.   1

WHAT'S INSIDE AND HOW TO USE THIS GUIDE.   4

STEP 1

What Are You Feeling?   5

STEP 2

What Is Your Heart's Desire?   13

STEP 3

What's the Point of a Relationship… for You?   22

STEP 4

Getting Yourself "Out There" — Without Forcing It.   28

STEP 5

Dealing With Rejection.   47

STEP 6

How To Know if It's "Right" ... Or Not.   55

STEP 7

Release Your Expectations.   63

MORE TIPS, MORE TOOLS

4 FAQs About the Challenges of Being Single.   66

WHAT'S NEXT?

Resources… to Keep Learning and Growing.   88

ABOUT THE AUTHOR   97

OTHER BOOKS BY THE AUTHOR   98

INDEX   100

DISCLAIMER

This book is a tool that can help you to navigate the challenges of being single and savor the dating adventure.

This book contains educational exercises and tips drawn from my career in the field of emotional wellness with over 30 years of experience. This book is for informational purposes only, and is not intended to diagnose or treat any illness, nor is it a substitute for professional or psychological advice, diagnosis, or treatment. Always consult a qualified health care professional before engaging in any new, self-help resource (such as this one) and with questions you may have about your health and wellbeing.

Any case material that may be alluded to in this book, including in articles, or in interviews [see Resources section] does not constitute guarantees of similar outcomes for the reader. No results can be promised, since everyone's personal development path is unique. Names and details have been changed for privacy.

Links inside this book to external websites are for informational purposes only. Linking does not imply endorsement of or affiliation with that site, its content, or any product or service it may offer.

All link URLs in this book are current at the time of printing. Link URLs may fail at some point if the page has been deleted or moved. The author assumes no responsibility or liability for broken links.

This concludes the disclaimer portion of this book.

Thank you. Enjoy this Guide ... and enjoy your life.

INTRODUCTION

With the Right Mindset and Practices, Finding True Love Can Be Truly Delightful

Welcome to The Life Guide on How to Navigate Being Single.

"Someone you haven't met yet is dreaming of adoring you."

—Danielle LaPorte

If you picked up a copy of this Guide, chances are, you might be feeling ...

- **Frustrated. Nervous.** Even a little ... **hopeless.**

   ("I've been single for so long ... is true, lasting love ever going to happen for me?")

- **Curious**, but **cautious**.

  ("I split up with somebody, and it hurt. I don't want to repeat the same patterns and mistakes.")

- **Curiosity**, tinged with **grief**.

  ("I lost someone dear to me. Can I really find true love, twice?")

Or something completely different.

Whatever you're feeling ... is what you're feeling. These feelings are not "good" or "bad."

But…

When it comes to savoring your time as a single person and connecting with the right person for you, certain feelings and attitudes are healthier and more productive than others.

(More on that, soon…)

This Guide can help you to:

— **Manage your feelings**

— **Shift into a positive frame of mind**

— **Find healthy ways to deal with "rejection"**

(because it doesn't have to be devastating…)

and

— Truly enjoy the adventure ahead

You deserve love.

Deep, permanent love.

From:

— Yourself.

And from:

— Someone else.

Let's begin!

What's Inside and How To Use This Guide

Inside this Life Guide, you'll find a series of steps to guide you through:

— **preparing** for

and

— **building**

the **loving, healthy relationship** you deserve.

Some steps include fill-in-the-blank worksheets.

Other steps contain scripts to help you through **potentially awkward conversations** – like those ones involving "**rejection**," a tricky subject.

Each step is designed to support you to not only:

— **Welcome the loving relationship you deserve into your life**,

but to also

— **Deepen your love for YOURSELF in the process**.

The Contents page of this Life Guide gave you a peek at what's ahead.

STEP 1

What Are You Feeling?

As a life coach and a psychologist, I almost always begin my sessions with a simple **emotional "check-in,"** to support the people I work with to connect to their feelings.

Why start there?

Because…

It's difficult to release the emotions that might be holding you back from creating what you want …

when you don't know what you're feeling.

Here's a **writing exercise** to:

get all those feelings out on the page.

Try not to:

— **over-think your answers**

or

—**worry if they sound:**

— "**positive**"

or

— "**negative**"

or even

— "**irrational**"

or

—"**silly.**"

Self-criticism is never okay.

Just express whatever you feel.

Without editing or being attentive to grammar.

Let the words flow…

Fill in the blanks:

I'm scared that I will never

_____

_____

_____

I'm nervous about trying

_____

_____

_____

I'm nervous about repeating

_____

_____

_____

I'm embarrassed / ashamed to admit that

_____

_____

_____

_____

Sometimes, I wonder if something is "wrong" with me, like

_____

_____

_____

_____

I feel like I'm running out of time to

_____

_____

_____

_____

I'm jealous of people who

_____

_____

_____

_____

But, I do feel hopeful when

_____

_____

_____

_____

Write ... and release.

If, after expressing your emotions on paper, you're still feeling a bit shaky (perhaps scared, nervous and / or embarrassed / ashamed) you might want to:

Take this self-expression exercise one step further, by releasing your emotional energy — safely and appropriately.

Here's how:

Set aside 5 - 10 minutes of uninterrupted time for yourself in a private space.

Then, take a pillow and gently hold it up to your face.

Now think about what made you scared, nervous and / or ashamed.

Feel these feelings.

Then release them by screaming into the pillow (it muffles the sound).

It may seem silly to scream — especially if you're not the sort of person who does that sort of thing very often, or ever!

But why not try it?

You may be surprised by how much relief you feel, as you release those pent-up emotions, safely.

All done?

Next,

Take a deep breath in

and

Affirm (in your mind):

"I accept whatever I'm feeling."

Then,

Exhale

and

Affirm (in your mind):

"I am letting go of the negative feelings that I don't need."

Once again:

Inhale deeply

and

Affirm, in your mind:

"I accept whatever I'm feeling."

Exhale

and

Affirm, in your mind:

"I am letting go of the negative feelings that I don't need."

Next,

Take one more deep breath, a bit more slowly.

Inhale

and

Hold your breath for a moment, counting to two. 1 ... 2.

Exhale

and

Push the air all the way out, like a big sigh. Ahhhhh.

Beautiful.

Now that you've **identified** (and **released**) some of your feelings, it's time for a **particularly exciting part of your dating adventure**:

Discovering your heart's desire.

STEP 2

What Is Your Heart's Desire?

It's always an exciting day when a client comes into my office — or hops on the phone with me — and says,

"I'm ready to start dating again!"

After a moment of celebration, I often begin by asking,

"What is your heart's desire?

What kind of relationship do you want to build?"

Sometimes, my client knows exactly what he or she is ready to build.

And that's wonderful.

With a clear vision in place, it's always much easier to create what you desire!

Other times, my client might be a little foggy.

("I don't know ... just, a good connection with someone, I guess?")

And other times, my client might know **exactly** what he or she desires ...

but feel **uncomfortable** saying the words, out loud.

Here's a story about what can happen when you're unable to express your heart's desire — and how to find the courage to say it:

Kristen shared with me her deep desire to meet the man of her dreams, and have children.

She strongly believed in the concept of marriage and raising a family.

To this end, she put a lot of energy into dating, and into tending to her physical and emotional health, so that she'd be in the best possible shape to create a family.

During one of our meetings, I asked her to share her goals out loud.

"Tell me how you would like your life to look — say, in two years."

Her reply,

"I want to meet 'the one' and have kids, and I want to be in a more satisfying career."

One of her most important goals was glaringly absent.

So I asked, gently:

"No marriage?"

Kristen was shocked that she hadn't included marriage.

"Oh, I definitely want that!" she said, with excitement.

*We then spent some time looking at **why** she had left "marriage" out of her goal list.*

She realized that:

as much as she "wanted" to be married, on a deeper, subconscious level, she didn't feel that she "deserved" to love and be loved in that way.

She also realized that

her lack of self-worth may have been causing her to subconsciously block her meeting Mr. Right.

"Maybe that's why it's taking so-o-o-o-o long," she said.

In time, we **reversed this negative self-perception**, changing

— I don't deserve"

to

— "I do."

Try this writing exercise to help you define your heart's desire — all of your wants, needs, hopes and dreams.

— For **yourself**,

and for

— the **two of you** as a **couple**.

Just like before, try not to

— **over-think** your answers

or

— **judge** them.

Your only job here is to be honest with yourself.

Fill in the blanks:

I desire a partner who

_____

_____

_____

_____

I desire a relationship that feels

_____

_____

_____

_____

When I wake up next to my partner, I want to feel

_____

_____

_____

_____

I desire a relationship where we build

_____

_____

_____

_____

I desire a relationship where we try

_____

_____

_____

_____

I desire a relationship where we have

_____

_____

_____

_____

I desire a relationship where we both love

_____

_____

_____

_____

I desire a relationship where we both prioritize

_____

_____

_____

_____

I desire a relationship where we're both committed to

_____

_____

_____

_____

More than anything, I desire

_____

_____

_____

_____

Read your list of desires out loud.

Are some of them hard to say?

For some people, this means they don't feel they deserve to have what they desire.

If that rings a bell, it can be helpful to take a look at the script that's playing in your mind — the one which says:

"You're not worthy."

Then reflect on how you learned to feel unworthy.

Typically, this has its roots in childhood.

Our caregivers / parents did the best they could, but sometimes we learned things that don't actually serve us.

It's helpful to understand where this script originated.

But if nothing comes to mind, that's okay.

Either way,

it's time to replace the "unworthy" script with one that is more true for you ... more loving.

One that says,

"I am worthy of love. I deserve what I desire."

STEP **3**

What's the "Point" of a Relationship, for You?

What's the "point" of a relationship?

It may seem like a silly question, but it's not.

The "point" of a relationship can be different for different people.

For your **best friend**, the "point" might be:

— to form a **strong, unified family** and raise **happy kids**.

For your **brother**, the "point" might be:

— to expose each other to **new experiences and adventures**, and challenge each other to grow.

For your **cousin**, the "point" might be:

to have someone to **enjoy life's many pleasures with.**

For your co-worker, the "point" might be:

to have **continual companionship** — an anchor, a refuge from the stormy world.

It's so important to clarify what the "point" is, for you.

So that you can have a clear idea of what you're seeking in a relationship — and what you're not.

Ideally, you'll be able to clearly express your "must-haves" in your online dating profile (if you're choosing that route) as well as face-to-face, on one of your early dates.

This will save BOTH of you a lot of:

- **time**

and

- **emotional energy**,

if this particular pairing is **not** a good fit.

Try this writing exercise to help you discover what the "point" of a relationship is for you, right now.

Fill in the blanks:

For me, the "point" of a relationship is

_____

_____

_____

_____

For me, the biggest mark of a "successful" relationship is

_____

_____

_____

_____

For me, a "good" relationship is one where both people

_____

_____

_____

Are you dating someone and your "points" are not matching up? Press pause.

If you and the person you're dating have dramatically different definitions about what a "good" relationship means and what the "point" of a relationship is, that could be a red flag.

You'll probably have trouble building a life together, because : ultimately, you'll have **different values** —

You won't want the same things.

But, if your definitions are aligned, you'll be much more likely to enjoy a beautiful, collaborative journey —

you will be building the same future, together.

Of course, **sharing a vision of the future** is just one component of a healthy relationship.

The second, vital component is that the two potential partners aren't bringing a lot of **"emotional baggage"** to the relationship.

("Baggage" = unresolved emotions from childhood, and possibly from past relationships as adults, leading to unhealthy patterns, today.)

If one (of both) of you have a lot of emotional baggage, this is likely to strain the relationship, as one (or both) will look to each other to fill your unmet emotional needs.

No one can resolve your emotional baggage, but you.

Not even the most loving, caring partner in the world.

(And vice versa.)

- **YOU need to resolve your unresolved emotions.**
- **YOUR PARTNER must resolve his or her unresolved emotions.**

Then, when the two of you come together in a relationship, two whole and healthy people are coming together to create a whole and healthy entity —

the relationship.

We'll revisit this idea of "emotional wholeness" in Step 6 of the Life Guide.

For now?

Just hold the idea in the back of your mind.

Stay open to discovering any unresolved emotions you might be holding onto — perhaps without even realizing it — so that soon, you can release them, fully, and become the best possible partner you can be.

Next?

Let's talk about **getting yourself "out there" in the dating world** — without forcing it.

STEP 4

Getting Yourself "Out There" — Without Forcing It.

If you do an internet search to see how many unmarried adults living in the United States of America, right now, you're likely to find that the numbers are astonishing.

Now, "unmarried" doesn't necessarily mean the same thing as "single" — but even so, the overall point is clear:

There are MILLIONS of people looking for love.

And worldwide, outside of the USA?

Billions.

This means the possibility that **there are so many wonderful people to meet, and there are so many ways to meet them.**

And no, you don't have to go online — but for many people it's an effective way to expand your options, instantly!

If you're feeling skittish about throwing yourself into the dating pool, start small and gently.

— Just go out somewhere new and unfamiliar.

Either alone, or with a supportive friend.

— You don't have to talk (or flirt) with anyone.

Just go and allow yourself to "be seen."

Exercise.

Make a list of:

— three places you'd like to go

or

— three activities you'd like to do…

either

— alone

or

— with a friend.

There's only one "rule" — the places or activities, on your list, must be out in the world (not at home in your pajamas! :)

I'd love to visit / do / try:

1.

_____

_____

2.

_____

_____

3.

_____

_____

Feeling stuck?

A simple tip:

Do an internet search using this phrase:

"10 free things to do in {name of your town or city here}."

You're almost guaranteed to find a great starter-list!

Want to explore the world of online dating?

If yes, pat yourself on the back for being willing to step out of your familiar comfort zone… and try something new.

As I mentioned a few moments ago, online dating doesn't feel "right" for everyone, and it's certainly not a "must-do."

But, many people have found it to be an incredible way to connect with people they might not meet any other way — and open themselves up to thousands of new possibilities, instantly.

In fact, these days I seem to be seeing, and talking to, more and more people, who met their parters online. It's no longer "taboo" — it's very common!

In the past, I had some reservations about the potential viability of relationships — and even marriages — where the partners and / or spouses meet each other online.

But it appears that in many cases, these couples find their relationships to be extremely satisfying — often more so, than those relationships that begin in traditional, offline venues."

An internet search of the most popular places to meet people, online is likely to yield a range of options and features including:

— being exposed to a considerable pool of potential connections.

— service in multiple countries and multiple different languages

(open to just about everyone in the world.)

— free trial sign-ups for a few days, to get a feel for how the service works. After that, you'll need a paid subscription to continue searching and sending messages to other users.

(Many people like the fact that some online dating services are NOT free, because the small monthly investment tends to filter out people who aren't really serious about connecting.)

Another online dating option can involve:

— meeting people at events, activities and clubs — some for singles, some for couples, and some for people who simply share common interests.

If you like the idea of "spontaneously" meeting someone at:

- a book club
- wine tasting

or

- on a bicycle ride

rather than

- at a "singles" event

this type of online dating service could be a great option for you.

And then there's the concept of a free dating site with a paid subscription option that gives you a bit more privacy — allowing you to peek at other people's profiles without them knowing.

I've heard from a number of people how much they enjoy this option when it comes to online dating.

It also helps that these individuals have a very positive attitude towards online dating, and are optimistic about their chances of connecting with someone they'll love.

Recently, a client shared with me about a relatively new dating site that's really "working" for them. It's based on a brilliantly simple concept:

— Post an activity you'd like to share with someone

"How about we ... head to a rock concert tonight? I've got an extra ticket!"

Or

"How about we ... walk our dogs through Central Park?"

Then...

Potential dates chime in to say,

"I'd love to!"

It's a matter of choosing someone you'd like to meet, and away you go!

Another client, who seriously wants to meet "Mr. Right!" Shared with me that she's loving a particular smartphone app that uses satellite technology to find potential matches in her immediate area/

This makes it easy to meet up for spontaneous, low-pressure dates.

— Swipe "like,"

and

— if they swipe "like" for you too,

it's a match!

(Interested? Do an internet search to learn more about how an app like this works. I've intentionally not linked to apps or online dating sites here, because it's a good warm up for you to do "surfing" to see what suits your particular tastes.)

Exercise:

Get emotionally ready to get "out there."

Whether you're gearing up to enter the world of online dating — or hoping to meet someone, offline — it's important to get emotionally ready for the experience, and **shift into a positive frame of mind.**

Here's a little "ritual" to help boost your mood and connect with the part of you that is excited, energized and hopeful about the adventure ahead:

1. **Dance!**

Put on your favorite music and move your body.

— Get ready to **get out of your present mood**

   (if it's a downer)

and into a

— **sexy, fun space**.

Country music always does that for me, but if that's not your taste, no biggie.

You might prefer a different type of pre-date mix, perhaps one with lots of upbeat indie rock.

Or

A mix of the top 50 sexiest songs of all time.

Or

Have some fun creating your own personalized soundtrack.

2. **Visualize!**

Take 5 - 10 minutes of uninterrupted time.

Get in a comfortable position, seated or lying down.

Close your eyes.

Visualize yourself all dressed up and ready for your date.

Take a moment to **appreciate** how beautiful / handsome you are.

Admire the image in your mind…

— Not only for **how you look**

But also because of

— **Who** you are

— The **type of person** you are

— Your **values**

— **Beliefs**

— **Morals**

— **The way you live** your live

With your eyes still closed, **say out loud**, to yourself:

"I like you. I love you, always."

Repeat out loud, a few times:

"I like you. I love you, always."

When you're ready,

— **Open your eyes**

and

— **Adjust to the light in your environment**.

With your eyes open,

— **Say out loud**:

"I like you. I love you, always."

Repeat out loud:

"I like you. I love you, always."

If you feel a **few butterflies in your stomach**, you may think you're nervous.

Keep in mind that what you're feeling may not be "nervousness," but **excitement**!

Or, a little bit of both.

That's healthy.

There is such as thing as **positive anxiety**. Just enough emotional energy to keep us:

— **Thinking** on our feet,

— **Primed** and **poised**,

And yes,

— **Excited** for what's next.

3. **Dab on some good feelings!**

Dab your wrists (and anywhere else on your body) with your favorite, feel-good perfume or cologne.

Or

Perhaps **a brand-new scent** that doesn't have any old memories tied to it.

Ever admired someone's perfume or cologne?

"Gee that fragrance smells heavenly! Which one is it?"

Ever wondered if there is a link between fragrance and feelings, both positive and negative?

You could conduct your own little study. Here's what you'll probably find:

Using a fragrance is a powerful way to shift your mood, very quickly.

Have you found your signature scent?

A scent that:

- **captures your essence**

and

- **compliments your personality**

(your preferences in the areas of food, music, clothing, etc)

while, at the same time

- **smells amazing!**

If not, spend some time **experimenting** with perfumes and / or colognes to find out what one's are best suited to you, or to some lucky person for whom you are considering giving a gift of a perfume or cologne.

Fast forward...

You now have a bottle of your favorite scent in your hand.

You dab some on your wrists.

You spray some around your neck, and even in your hair...

Let the pleasant scent lift your mood and relax you.

Then ...

Close your eyes.

Breathe in deeply and as you do, **think** to yourself:

"I am ready for this experience."

Exhale fully, **thinking**:

"I am beautiful / attractive / handsome."

Breathe in deeply and as you do, **think**:

"I am confident."

Exhale fully, thinking:

"I am lovable."

4. **Dress to impress (yourself!)**

Wear something you love.

Have a lucky charm, or favorite piece of jewelry?

Go for it.

Whatever it takes to make yourself feel as light, happy and energized as possible.

Go for it.

Exercise:

Give yourself 5 first date fashion tips, from the perspective of the person you're going to meet for the first time.

The date... the time... the place... it's all set up.

Now that proverbial question —

"What shall I wear?"

Close your eyes for a moment.

Imagine the person you're about to meet is, let's say, sitting at a table a in the restaurant where the two of you have decided to meet — waiting for you.

Imagine yourself walking through the revolving door at the entrance of the restaurant, and then...

You see your date sitting at the table.

And

He sets eyes on you, for the very first time.

Visualize that your first date sees at least 5 fabulous things about you.

Now, open your eyes

And

When you're ready, complete this next writing exercise

Fill in the blanks:

The 5 fabulous things that my date sees about me are

1.
_____

_____

_____

_____

2.
_____

_____

_____

3.
_____

_____

_____

_____

4.
_____

_____

_____

_____

5.
_____

_____

_____

_____

Congrats! You've just given yourself 5 fashion tips for your first date.

If you'd like, you could continue this visualization exercise, followed by a "Fill in the blanks" writing exercise by giving yourself more style tips for different kinds of dates —

- first dates

- second dates

And or

- meeting the parents

And

- other scenarios that come to mind!

Keep in mind that you are unique.

That means: No one has the same personal style as you do.

So don't let:

— Fashion trends

And / or

— What other people will think

Be your style guide.

Instead, keep your personal style

- **Authentic**

And

- **Unique**

And

- **Cultivate your own positive self-image.**

Remember:

At the end of the day, choose something that YOU love to wear ... regardless of what the "style experts" say.

A few final thoughts for your pre-date ritual:

You deserve to:

— **take excellent care of yourself**

— **love and respect yourself**

and

— feel beautiful and attractive ...

no matter what the outcome of the date may be.

Going on a date may feel scary, at times, but consider asking yourself this:

"What's the worst than can happen on this date?"

The worst case scenario is that:

— You'll have **a pleasant conversation**

and

— Get to practice **being "present"** with another person (who is likely just as nervous as you!).

The best case scenario?

You'll make a beautiful connection. And see where it goes!

Next?

Let's talk about everyone's least favorite topic: "rejection." (And how to deal with it.)

STEP 5

Dealing With "Rejection"

One of the biggest fears that has held a lot of my clients back from getting "out there" and dating again is:

the fear of rejection.

People often think:

If he / she rejects me, it means:

— *I'm not worthy.*

It means:

— *I'm unattractive.*

It means

— there's something wrong with me.

But that is completely untrue.

Rejection is not personal.

It's about "preference," not "worthiness."

Other people have preferences.

You can have preferences, too.

Once you recognize that fact, then being "rejected" — or having to "reject" someone — becomes **a lot less overwhelming**.

You can take the heightened emotions out of the situation, and simply remind yourself:

"It's OK to have preferences."

Exercise

If you've been "rejected" …

Here's an **affirmation** to say to yourself.

Being rejected doesn't mean that I'm

It simply means that this person has a different preference.

It's healthy for me to have preferences, too!

I'm grateful for the time we shared together.

I'm grateful for their honesty with me.

And ...

I'm excited for whatever's next.

If you need to "reject" someone else ...

this script can help you say "no thanks" to a 1st (or 2nd) date:

Hello (person's name),

I enjoyed meeting you / chatting with you on the phone / chatting online, and I especially liked hearing about

---

(describe something they are passionate about: their job, their travel plans, their hobbies.)

I'm flattered that you want to go out on a date / second date, and I think you're

---

(describe one of their positive qualities).

But I don't feel that we're a potential match.

I hope that you'll find what you're looking for, and I wish you the best of luck.

(your name here)

A few more words on "rejection" (and your upbringing).

If being rejected triggers **an intense emotional reaction** —

— a **hot flush**

— a **cold sweat**

— sharp **anger** towards your date

("how could s/he dump me!")

or yourself (even **self-loathing**) —

("I'm not attractive,")

("I'm not likable")

or

— **insecurity**

that **sticks** with you for hours, days or weeks

("What's wrong with me? Why doesn't s/he want to go out with me?")

— you may want to look at these emotional reactions, closer.

Why?

When this happens, it often suggests that there was a need in childhood that was not satisfied.

When you experience rejection, it can bring you back to that needy childhood place. Hence: the **exaggerated (intense) reaction**.

It's important to resolve these excessive feelings — so that you can be "baggage-free" and truly enjoy your dating adventure, and enjoy healthier relationships with yourself and others.

Exercise:

Some steps that can help to release emotional baggage around "rejection":

1. First, one way to try to **pin-point what may have happened that gave rise to the distorted emotions**, is by asking yourself:

"When have I felt this way before?"

Example:

One person who was really angry at his date for "rejecting" him, realized that he was re-living the guilt and frustration from all the times that his mom didn't pay attention to him.

2. Next, **release the pent-up feelings** you are holding inside.

(Perhaps by screaming into a pillow, like we did in Step 1 of this Guide.)

3. Now that you have released some of those feelings, you can **rewrite the script** that's playing in your mind.

You might write, think or say to yourself:

"That was then. This is now.

I am no longer that young child who was starved for

_____

_____

_____

_____

I can heal that part of me that is still craving

_____

_____

_____

_____

I can tell the child who I once was, that

"I love you

and that

Everything will be OK."

4. Can't figure out where your pent-up emotions are coming from?

That's OK. You can still release those feelings, even if you're unsure of their origin.

And then, you can **write, think or say to yourself:**

"For whatever reason, I am experiencing strong emotions around rejection.

But I don't have to feel this way.

I can choose to feel differently.

I am a loving person who deserves to be loved.

If someone chooses not to date me, that's all right.

It just means we're not the best fit.

My worth is not dependent on someone wanting to date me.

I would have liked it to work out, and it's OK to be disappointed that it did not.

But now I can move on.

I look forward to more dates and I'm excited to meet someone amazing, who desires me just as much as I desire them, and wants to build the same kind of future, together.

I know that person is dreaming of me, just as I'm dreaming of them."

Resolving emotional "baggage" around "rejection" is important.

If these kinds of feelings remain unresolved, your dating experience may very well be burdened by stress and overwhelm.

And eventually?

You might find yourself too overwhelmed to keep trying.

So do what you need to do, and if you need extra help from a qualified healthcare professional? Don't be afraid to seek it out.

To paraphrase (and slightly tweak!) a classic quote from The Buddha:

"Rejection is inevitable. Suffering is optional!"

Next?

We'll talk about **how to know if a particular relationship is "right" ... or not**.

STEP 6

How to know if it's "right" ... or not.

A lot of people agonize over whether someone is "right" for them, or not.

But…

choosing and committing to a partner is not a "mysterious" thing.

It can be simple.

If you

— **value the same things** ...

— **want to build the same kind of future** ...

and

are both coming into the relationship as **whole, healthy people** (without lots of unresolved baggage).

Then...

this match has the **potential to be a good one**.

It's not about "perfection."

The person you're dating doesn't have to be "perfect."

But when it comes to their qualities, the **positive needs to outweigh the negative** — at least, as far as your preferences are concerned.

It's important that you are able to feel confident saying:

"I could see myself building a life with this person, just as they are, without feeling like I'm short-changing myself."

True colors, revealed.

Remember, also, that **it takes time to get to know someone**.

You each have lived a whole lifetime separately.

You don't have to spend the equivalent of a lifetime getting to know each other, but...

- Take it slow.

- Don't force it.

It's common for each person to be on their **best behavior**, especially in the early stages of dating.

But in time, **true colors tend to emerge** — especially during times of **stress**.

You need to see those true colors in order to make an informed decision about whether this relationship is "right" or not.

Values, aligned.

Look back at your definition of a "good" relationship" and what the "point" of a relationship is, from Step 3 of this Guide.

When it feels appropriate, have a conversation with the person you're dating.

Ask about their definitions of those same terms, and listen.

Are you both on the same page?

Or close to it?

If so, great!

— Stop worrying,

— keep getting to know one another,

and

— see what unfolds ...

Again,

— **without rushing**.

Take your sweet time (...especially with sex).

Relationships that begin as friendships are the ones that tend to succeed, long-term.

So be friends, first.

Then, the foundation of your relationship will be **compatibility**, not (just) sexual chemistry.

Enjoy the sexual attraction. But ...

that doesn't mean you need to act on it, immediately. You might even want to make a promise yourself that you won't act on it, immediately.

Enjoy the butterflies in your stomach as you see your date walking towards you.

Enjoy the feeling of your heart beating super-fast when you see a text message from them.

But ... wait.

A question I'm often asked is,

"Does that mean no touching, hand-holding, or kissing?"

I usually reply with a question:

"Imagine spending time alone with someone you find attractive, and you start touching and kissing.

Are you going to be able to stop?

Wouldn't that be a temptation that's very hard to resist?"

If you "jump into bed" too quickly, it will probably feel thrilling at first, but invariably it's a distraction from really getting to know someone on a deeper level.

You might regret having sex too soon (sadly, many people do).

But there's little chance that you'll regret giving yourselves the gift of a slow, unhurried courtship.

Plus, waiting and building slowly towards sex can make the eventual experience SO much better!

Feeling ... unsatisfied?

Some people end perfectly good relationships because they have unmet emotional needs that they expect their partner to satisfy, for them.

They feel empty and unsatisfied, so they cut things off.

("S/he wouldn't give me _____, so I figured it wasn't right.")

That's a shame, because as we've discussed earlier in this Guide, **some needs can ONLY be filled by YOU.**

A story:

Here's a story about a woman who wanted her potential partner to meet one of her emotional needs — but ultimately realized that she needed to fulfill that need, herself.

On their second date, Mike asked Cheryl:

"What do you think makes a relationship healthy?""

"For starters," she said, "I want you to respect me and I want you to be patient with me."

Those are great "wants."

Except that Cheryl didn't respect herself and was very impatient with herself.

Cheryl needed to trade these unloving behaviors for self-love.

Mike cannot (nor should he be asked to) satisfy her emotional neediness.

This would put a tremendous strain on their relationship.

For Cheryl and Mike to experience a healthy relationship, both need to be emotionally whole.

Otherwise, one or both of them will be **looking to each other for the emotional nurturance** that they need to give to themselves.

You deserve to have a loving relationship.

But it starts with **committing to loving yourself**, right now.

Which means:

- appreciating yourself,

- being kind,

- fair

and

- honest with yourself,

- listening to yourself,

and

- accepting and trusting yourself.

People who love and respect themselves tend to have healthier relationships.

Why?

Because they tend to attract people who take good care of themselves and feel worthy of love, too.

Next?

We'll talk about how to **release expectations** of what your ideal partner should look like and be.

STEP 7

Release your expectations

Have you ever planned a party, a project or date with a great deal of specificity …

— every detail in place, just so —

only to have it wind up **differently than you expected**?

— Maybe it rained during your outdoor picnic,

or

— ants descended upon your meal.

— Maybe the project fell behind schedule,

and

— you had to hire someone new,

or

— change the whole timeline.

— Maybe your date was a tall brunette,

not the

— petite redhead you'd always imagined in your fantasies.

You probably felt disappointed, sad or annoyed.

That's because:

"expectations" invariably lead to disappointment.

It's great to have "desires" — to be clear about what you want and the values you hold — but remember that "the one" might arrive in **different "packaging"** than you expect, or in a **different setting** than you expect, or even at a **different time** than you expect.

Be curious, playful and open to unexpected possibilities.

Say to yourself, within your mind:

"I am ready to receive exactly what I want --

or something better.

Surprise me."

- **Clarify** your desires.

- **Expand** your horizons.

But…

- **Release** your "expectations."

Most of all,

dial up the amount of love and care that you give to yourself.

Why?

A well-loved woman (or man) is extremely attractive.

Choose love.

Step out into the world.

And **love will find you.**

MORE TIPS, MORE TOOLS

4 FAQs About the Challenges of Being Single

Now that you've read Step 1 through Step 7 of this Life Guide, (which means that you have more tools in your dating toolbox, so to speak), you may already be feeling more hopeful and excited to get out there! Here are even more tips and tools to continue your journey to handle the challenges of being single and savor the dating adventure..

Read on for my answers[1] to some of the more typical questions I've been asked over the past 3+ decades as I've helped people who were single learn how to deal with the emotions that were holding them back from **finding true love** — and **make dating FUN again!**

---

[1] The questions and answers are summarized here, to maximize your learning experience.

Question No. 1 — Pessimistic about having success with dating

Replacing Self-Judgement With Confidence

Over the past 7 years I've had 3 relationships that lasted between 6 months to 4 years. Nothing worked out. The most recent one ended 4 months ago.

Two relationships were good ones — at least I thought so. The third one was no good from the get-go (he ignored me, mostly, but he had a lot of status, and that's why I tagged along at his side.)

The two "good" relationships ended mostly because I wanted more (commitment), and the other half was happy to keep things as they were.

I'm 35 and I want to have children, so I needed to move on and see if I could find someone to fall in love with, who is willing to commit.

I've been dating a bit during the last 4 months but I've lost my enthusiasm. I feel like I'm just no good at this dating scene... actually I don't think I really like it... but that could be partly because I feel like I'm such a loser when it comes to dating — I mean, let's face it, I've had 3 relationships and NONE of them worked out!

And I must have been in some dream world to think that two of these relationships were good ones, when they really weren't good for me (no commitment) even though my partners were happy.

How can I get motivated again to date and be open and optimistic about meeting "the one?"

Response:

Yes, more often than not **finding true love takes great patience**.

But

— it's less likely to happen

and

— more likely to take a lot longer

if

— we're filled with self-judgement

("I'm such a loser when it comes to dating")

and

— we lack confidence

("I'm not good at this dating scene.")

It's not surprising that you feel like your motivation "has gone south" so to speak.

When our self-talk is negative, it's as if we're going against our true nature —

which is positive. When this happens, it drains our energy.

The result?

We feel like we have **no motivation.**

We feel like we have **no energy, no zest, no adrenaline** to take action and do what we need to do to get closer to achieving our goals (to date, in this instance).

It would be akin to filling up your bathtub with water, but there's no stopper on the drain.

The result?

Instead of the tub being filled with water, the water drains out.

Remember:

No experience (including a dating experience) is wasted, if we learn from it.

This means —

When it comes to your past relationships, you might want to spend some time looking at:

- **Why** you chose the "partners" that you did

- **Why** you stayed in those relationships as long as you did,

and

- **Why** those relationships didn't work out.

Why is doing this type of exercise a good idea?

Because then, when it comes to dating and choosing a potential partner...

you'll better equipped to make different choices next time,

and

you're less likely to end up in the same type of relationships that you did in the past — ones that didn't work out.

Once you learn the lessons that need to be learned from your past dating experiences, you will also be **more confident** about your ability to be have more **successful** dating experiences in the future.

In essence, you'll find it easier to...

- **Replace self-judgement**

("I'm such a loser when it comes to dating")

with

- **Self-confidence**

("I'm good at navigating this dating scene.")

Exercise Number 1:

Fill in the blanks:

You can do the next two exercises for each of your past relationships.

Try not to:

— **Overthink**

— **Overanalyze**

Or

— Let **self-judgement** cause you to **edit** your true response.

As you do this exercise, also keep in mind that:

There's nothing wrong with being ignorant. It just means that there is something that we haven't yet learned or mastered.

And,

There's nothing wrong with making a mistake. Yes, there are consequences for choices, and sometimes the price we pay for making a mistake can be steep. But…

If mistakes were not ok, pencils wouldn't have erasers.

When it comes to my past relationship, I chose that partner because…

_____

_____

_____

_____

I stayed in that relationship as long as I did, because…

_____

_____

_____

_____

That relationship didn't work out because…

_____

_____

_____

_____

Exercise Number 2:

Fill in the blanks:

When it comes to my past dating relationship, I have learned...

_____

_____

_____

_____

In my next dating relationship, I will chose a partner who is...

_____

_____

_____

_____

In my next dating relationship, I will only continue to stay in it, if...

_____

_____

_____

_____

Question No. 2 — Ashamed about being single

Replacing Embarrassment With Self-Acceptance

I'm in my late 30's. All my friends are married (some of them have kids) or paired up with someone. I knew quite a few of them when they were single.

I want to meet someone and get married...

I've wanted that for years... but it just hasn't happened yey.

I've dated on and off, and lived with someone for a while, but it didn't go anywhere permanent.

I like socializing with my friends and we do quite of lot of that (even some traveling together), but because I'm the only one who is single, I don't contribute much to the conversation — I feel like I have nothing to say...

I can't talk about my marriage because I don't have one.

I can't talk about my partner because I don't have one.

It's not that I feel sorry for myself... I'm just so embarrassed that, at my age, I'm still single.

I also worry that my friends are getting tired of me because I don't contribute to the conversations. I don't think that's fun for them.

I don't want to stop spending time with my friends but how can I continue to "socialize" when I have nothing to say?

Response:

Keep in mind that there's no requirement or necessity that in order to socialize and converse with people, we need to have similar experiences to the ones that they have.

Think about that for a moment...

Yet that's the very standard that you're imposing on yourself because you've concluded that just because you're not married, you have nothing to offer to a conversation which includes people who are married.

To the contrary...

— Every person (including you) **matters**, regardless of their experiences.

— Every person (including you) is capable of being a **good listener**, regardless of their experiences.

—Every person (including you) is capable of **empathy for someone else**, regardless of their experiences.

And

— Every person (including you) **deserves to speak** and **be heard**, regardless of their experiences.

Equally important...

There's nothing shameful about being single.

There's nothing shameful about not having met "the one" yet.

With that said…

If you choose to replace:

— being **ashamed**

with

— **self-acceptance**

You may very well find that you have lots to share with your friends — about your:

- life
- work
- interests
- goals
- dreams

plus

- anything else that you'd like to share

And

You may very well find that **your friends enjoy what you share**, and **find it interesting**, and **stimulating**.

Why?

Because

— True friends care about us, **unconditionally**.

— True friends **don't place limits** on what we can and cannot share with them.

— True friends **don't judge us** or **put us down** for not having achieved what they have (i.e., you're single, your friends are married.)

But…

Being a true friend starts with you. The more you become a true friend to yourself, the more accepting you are likely to be of yourself, and where you are at in your life.

Then what others think of you — or what you may be worrying that they are thinking of you — is likely to be a non-issue for you.

Why?

Because…

- **When we accept ourselves, we are at ease with ourselves.**

- **When we are at ease with ourselves, there's no room for self-judgement (which fuels shame and embarrassment).**

- **When we don't judge ourselves, we don't tend to worry that others will judge us.**

Sounds like you're a caring, sensitive friend with a lot to offer.

Enjoy your friends…

And may you have much success with dating.

Question No. 3 — Discomfort with small talk

Replacing Insecurity With Confidence

I'm 25 and I've been dating different people. I'm not ready to "settle down" with a life partner yet, but if I meet a life long partner, that is fine.

What I'm having trouble with, is making small talk on the first or second date, and sometimes even the third date.

I freeze up and my words just don't come out...

It's not that I don't have things to say... and when I'm with friends, and I feel comfortable, I have all kinds of things to say — but there's something about dating and not knowing the person I'm talking to very well, that makes me freeze.

When I'm not in a new situation and I know the people I'm talking to, and we have things in common, I'm really comfortable talking and my ideas and words come out smoothly.

But in a new situation, when I don't know the person — or, now that I think about it — when I have to do something like public speaking (doesn't matter if the audience is big or small) I'm uncomfortable.

I'm worried that my difficulty with small talk will be such a problem that I won't want to date anymore. What can I do about this?

Response:

It's good to hear that you're comfortable chatting with friends that you have things in common with you.

So you've narrowed your insecurity about small talk to people you don't really know — be that one-on-one dating, or in a more public setting in front of small or large groups.

Generally speaking, the emotion that is at the root of insecurity is **fear**.

This could be any type of fear, or a combination of fears.

Examples:

— Fear of sounding stupid.

— Fear of not being good enough.

— Fear of not being liked.

— Fear of rejection.

— Worry (fear) of what someone is going to think.

— And any other fear that comes to mind.

(Note to reader: At this point in my response to this question, I outlined an exercise for releasing fear safely and appropriately, The exercise was similar to the "scream into the pillow" exercise that is included in Step 1 of this life guide.)

Exercise Number 2:

If you don't feel quite ready to scream into a pillow (initially, some people feel silly at the thought of doing this, but once they do it they see how effective it is), here's another exercise that many people have found helpful.

Fill in the blanks:

Just write whatever comes to your mind. Take as much time, and use as much space, as you want. **There are no wrong answers.**

When I'm just beginning to date someone, I feel uncomfortable with small talk because...

_____

_____

_____

_____

When I'm just beginning to date someone, I don't know what to say because...

_____

_____

_____

_____

When I'm just beginning to date someone, my biggest fear/s is / or are...

_____

_____

_____

_____

Now that you have some understanding and insight about why you're uncomfortable with small talk and the early stages of dating, it's time for some **affirmations**.

Try these three self-affirming statements:

1. When I'm just beginning to date someone, I feel comfortable with small talk because I am curious to get to know my date.

2. When I'm just beginning to date someone, I know what to say because I'm interested in getting to know my date and what he or she has to share

3. When I'm just beginning to date someone, I feel confident I can handle the conversation intelligently and gracefully.

As for your discomfort about public speaking, the exercises that I have outlined in my response to your question (Exercise 1: Releasing fear safely and appropriately, Exercise 2: Fill-in-the blanks writing exercise, and the self-affirming affirmations) can be useful.

You might also want to take a look at the article that I wrote on this subject. It offers tips to manage this fear that prevents a lot of people from achieving their potential.

The article is called:

Terrified of Public Speaking? How to Get the Words Flowing
— Published online in The Huffington Post.

http://www.huffingtonpost.com/dr-suzanne-gelb/terrified-of-public-speaking-how-to-get-the-words-flowing_b_5841136.html

Question No. 4 — Hoping he'll change his mind

Learning To Let Go of Holding Onto the Past

About 6 years ago, a relationship that I was deeply invested in, ended. I was blind-sided by the sudden ending...

I never expected it. (Perhaps more accurate to say, I didn't really expect it. There were some warning signs that all was not rosy in paradise, but nothing that I thought wouldn't blow over. And when it happened, it came as such a shock — as if I never expected it.)

This relationship had lasted for around 4 years. Even as I'm writing this, it's hard for me to believe it's totally over. There was so much good between us... I'm still not totally sure what caused it to come to a screeching halt. Most of the time, I blame myself —

Maybe I was too busy... maybe I wasn't attentive enough... if only I'd lost more weight, sooner... if only I had been more patient... and on and on and on.

But it's clear he's moved on. He has a new girlfriend, and even a baby. But I still keep hoping that he'll come back to me — that he'll change his mind, realize how good we were together... and that nothing can come close to what we shared.

Because of that, I haven't dated in the past 6 years. I'm not getting any younger, and I want to get married, but I keep hoping he'll call me any day, and tell me he wants to get back together.

But the days, months and years are passing by, and I'm not dating or getting any closer to finding a partner. How to I move forward with my life — with or without him?

Response:

It's a good sign that you're asking the question about how to move forward.

It suggests that you're **not satisfied** with holding onto the past, if it means getting nowhere in the present… and therefore, possibly thwarting your dreams and goals for the future.

It's a good sign that you're not satisfied with holding onto the past… if it means **putting yourself on on hold in the present,** and again, possibly thwarting your dreams and goals for the future.

Sometimes, we spend so much time seeing the glass as half empty, rather than half full, that we lose sight of our own self-worth and self-respect.

We **lose sight of the fact** that:

— **We deserve more** than to just sit around and wait, and hope that maybe, just maybe… someone will change his or her mind

We **lose sight of the fact** that:

— We deserve more than to spend our days pining away for what was, and could have been, and for what might be… maybe…

We **lose sight of the fact** that:

— **We are special**, smart, loving and lovable.

We **lose sight of the fact** that:

— We have a lot of love to give and to receive…

and that

— There are plenty of wonderful people on this planet, and perhaps even someone else who we would want to love, and who would love us back…

and as such,

We're being unfair to ourselves to keep waiting and waiting for that one person from the past — who we thought really loved us — and who we hope will, someday, love us again…

So yes, **your question is timely**…

Yes, **you're right about wanting to move forward.**

It's time.

You're worth it.

You deserve it.

You have the ability to reach deep within yourself to find the courage to do it.

To **take that first step**.

To **go out on that first date**.

And when you do…

Be ready to experience is sense of **freedom**, and **lightness** and **love** for yourself, like never before.

Because…

By letting go of the past, you have taken the first step to open the door to the beautiful future of your dreams.

WHAT'S NEXT?

Resources... To Keep Learning and Growing

I hope you've enjoyed this Life Guide. It is "technically" complete, but I wanted to give you some **more resources on dating, love and self-care (because when you love, respect and take care of yourself, you're more likely to attract a partner who is similarly like-minded and therefore, compatible)** ... in case you'd like to continue the learning and the growing with me.

Here are some of my favorites — articles I've authored,[2] books I've written, and inspiring insights that I shared when I was interviewed by a reporter from the Weekend Today Show, to savor at your leisure.

Enjoy!

---

[2] Except where otherwise noted, all articles referenced in this section were published online.

Dating

Had Your Heart Broken? 21 Reasons To Start Dating Again
— Published on Mind Body Green.

http://www.mindbodygreen.com/0-15548/had-your-heart-broken-21-reasons-to-start-dating-again.html

Two Scripts That Can Help You Release Expectations, Relax and Show Up At Your Best On a First Date
— Published on The Huffington Post.

https://www.huffpost.com/entry/release-expectations-relax-and-show-up-on-a-first-date_b_6187136

4 Ways to Deal With An Office Crush
— Published in Dr. Gelb's column, "Be Well At Work," on The Muse.

https://muse.cm/2ilmk7H

7 Questions To Ask Before You Start A Rebound Relationship
— Published on Mind Body Green.

http://www.mindbodygreen.com/0-17955/7-questions-to-ask-before-you-start-a-rebound-relationship.html

Dating With Kids: Are Your Children Ready To Meet Your New Sweetheart?
— Published on The Huffington Post.

https://bit.ly/1FKl3vu

Why "Certain People" Make Us Feel Completely Insane And How To Reclaim Our "Zen."
— Published on Positively Positive.

https://bit.ly/2HOCdAg

Helping Your Teen Make Healthy Choices: About Dating And Intimacy
— A Life Guide written by Dr. Gelb.

https://amzn.to/2YU5MWF

3 Ways to Stop Your Teen From Making Risky Choices About Dating and Sex
— Published on The Huffington Post.

https://bit.ly/2WyNDAd

Why I Still Believe People Can Change
— Published on Positively Positive.

http://www.positivelypositive.com/2014/12/15/why-i-still-believe-that-people-can-change/

Sick Of Flaking Out? How To Start Keeping Your Word
— Published in Mind Body Green.

http://www.mindbodygreen.com/0-17050/sick-of-flaking-out-how-to-start-keeping-your-word.html

"Just Believe." How I Learned To Trust In The Universe, Even When All Hope Seemed Lost
— Published in Positively Positive.

http://www.positivelypositive.com/2015/03/26/just-believe-how-i-learned-to-trust-in-the-universe-even-when-all-hope-seemed-lost/

Feeling Phone-verwhelmed? 5 Tips To Help You Create A Healthier, Happier Relationship With Your Smartphone
— Published in Dr. Gelb's column, "All Grown Up," on Psychology Today.

https://www.psychologytoday.com/blog/all-grown/201508/feeling-phone-verwhelmed

Don't Feel Like Exercising? 3 Steps To Get You Off The Couch
— Published in Dr. Gelb's column, "All Grown Up," on Psychology Today.

https://www.psychologytoday.com/blog/all-grown/201505/don-t-feel-exercising-3-steps-get-you-the-couch

Ashamed of how you look in a swimsuit? Women: Please Read This
— Published on The Huffington Post.

https://www.huffpost.com/entry/post_n_5541682

Obsessing Over Wrinkles? Depressed About Aging? — 5 Questions To Help You Re-Focus On What Really Matters
— Published in Dr. Gelb's column, "All Grown Up," on Psychology Today.

https://www.psychologytoday.com/blog/all-grown/201502/obsessing-over-wrinkles-depressed-about-aging

Love

The Love Tune-Up: How to Amp Up the Love That's Naturally Inside You to Enjoy Happy, Healthy Relationships — A 14-Day Course That Can Change Your Life

https://amzn.to/2XQ7190

Welcome Home: Release Addictions and Return to Love

https://amzn.to/2vwXmIa

5 Ways to Stop Yourself from Eating When You're not Hungry
— Published on Psych Central.

http://psychcentral.com/blog/archives/2014/10/30/5-ways-to-stop-yourself-from-eating-when-youre-not-hungry/

Learning To Feed My Hungry Heart: My Journey From Bingeing To Wholeness
— Published in Dr. Gelb's column, "All Grown Up" on Psychology Today.

https://www.psychologytoday.com/intl/blog/all-grown/201904/learning-feed-my-hungry-heart

Stressed Out at Work? How to Cope -- Without Turning to Food or Booze
— Published on The Huffington Post.

https://www.huffpost.com/entry/stressed-out-at-work-how_n_6711034

Self-Care

You Are The Best Investment You'll Ever Make
— Published in Dr. Gelb's column, "All Grown Up" on Psychology Today.

https://www.psychologytoday.com/blog/all-grown/201511/you-are-the-best-investment-youll-ever-make

6 Self-Sabotaging Habits You Need To Drop Right Now
— Published on Mind Body Green.

https://www.mindbodygreen.com/0-14014/6-selfsabotaging-habits-you-need-to-drop-right-now.html

The Greatest Cheerleader One Can Have — Lives Within: How To Stay Strong When Not Everyone Is Cheering for our Success.
— Published in Dr. Gelb's column, "All Grown Up" on Psychology Today.

https://www.psychologytoday.com/us/blog/all-grown/201902/the-greatest-cheerleader-person-can-have-lives-within

If You Want to Make Tomorrow Less Stressful—Start Tonight
— Published in Dr. Gelb's column, "Be Well At Work, on The Muse.

https://www.themuse.com/advice/if-you-want-to-make-tomorrow-less-stressfulstart-tonight

How to Succeed Everywhere: 10 Tips for Balance at Work, Home, in Relationships
— Written by Shelby Marra, published online on NBC's Today.

https://www.today.com/health/how-become-high-achieving-woman-work-your-relationship-parent-t33071

Side note: As my colleague, friend, and gifted writing teacher, Alex Franzen said: *"THIS IS AMAZING! Being interviewed by a reporter from NBC's Today Show? Uh, that's the big leagues!"*

Yes, that's what happened. Shelby Marra with NBC's Today Show in New York, requested an interview with me so that she could write this article featuring me, for TODAY.com's Successful Women series.

How Successful People Do More in 24 Hours Than the Rest of Us Do in a Week
— Published on Newsweek; also published on The Muse.

https://www.newsweek.com/career/how-successful-people-do-more-24-hours-rest-us-do-week

Side note: The Muse is an online platform that attracts more than 75 million people each year, to help them be at the top of their game at work.

I'm honored to have received the praise below, from Adrian Granzella Larssen, Editor-in-Chief, in response to an article that I wrote for The Muse:

"Wow! This is fantastic stuff. You're clearly incredible at what you do, and I'm so thrilled to share your advice with our audience!"

You Want Couple's Counseling But Your Partner Does Not. Are You Doomed?
— Published on Dr. Gelb's column, "All Grown Up" on Psychology Today.

https://www.psychologytoday.com/blog/all-grown/201504/you-want-couple-s-counseling-your-partner-does-not

Why Positive Affirmations Don't Always Work (And What Does)
— Published on Tiny Buddha.

http://tinybuddha.com/blog/why-positive-affirmations-dont-always-work-and-what-does/

Why People Resist Seeking Therapy
— Published on Dr. Gelb's column, "All Grown Up" on Psychology Today.

https://www.psychologytoday.com/blog/all-grown/201510/why-people-resist-seeking-therapy

"What Actually Happens During A Therapy Session?"...
And 6 other common questions about psychotherapy
— Published on Dr. Gelb's column, "All Grown Up" on Psychology Today.

https://www.psychologytoday.com/blog/all-grown/201512/what-actually-happens-during-therapy-session

ABOUT THE AUTHOR

Dr. Suzanne Gelb, Ph.D., J.D. is a psychologist, life coach and author. For 3+ decades, she has helped people learn to manage the emotions that were holding them back from finding true love, and make dating FUN again!, using tools like the ones in this book.

Dr. Gelb's inspiring insights on emotional wellness have been featured on more than 200 radio programs, 260 TV interviews, and online on Time, Newsweek, Forbes, Psychology Today, The Huffington Post, NBC's Today, Positively Positive, Mind Body Green, The Muse and many other places, as well.

As a contributing writer to the Huffington Post, Dr. Gelb has written articles on dating, including, **Two Scripts That Can Help You Release Expectations, Relax and Show Up At Your Best On a First Date**, and **Dating With Kids: Are Your Children Ready To Meet Your New Sweetheart?** Her powerful article, **Had Your Heart Broken? 21 Reasons To Start Dating Again**, was published on Mind Body Green.

Dr. Gelb believes that it is never too late to become the person — or partner — you want to be. Strong. Confident. Calm. Creative. Free of all of the burdens that have held you back — no matter what happened in the past.

OTHER BOOKS BY THE AUTHOR

It Starts With You – How to Raise Happy, Successful Children by Becoming the Best Role-Model You Can Possibly Be. A Guidebook For Parents.

How to Get Your Kids to Cooperate and Help Them Become the Best Grown-Ups They Can Be. (A Life Guide.)

Helping Your Teen Make Healthy Choices About Dating and Sex. (A Life Guide.)

How to Get Ready to Be a Parent and Be the Best Mom or Dad You Can Possibly Be. (A Life Guide.)

How to Forgive the One Who Hurt You Most. (A Life Guide.)

How to Deal With People Who Drive You Absolutely Nuts. (A Life Guide.)

Aging With Grace, Strength and Self-Love. (A Life Guide.)

The Love Tune-Up: How to Amp Up the Love That's Naturally Inside You to Enjoy Happy, Healthy Relationships.

How to Rekindle That Spark and Create the Relationship and Sex Life That You Want. (A Life Guide.)

How to Find Work That You Love When You're Stuck in a Job That You Hate. (A Life Guide.)

How to Reach Your Ideal Weight Through Kindness, Not Craziness. (A Life Guide.)

Welcome Home: Release Addictions and Return to Love.

How to Care for Yourself When You're a Caregiver for Somebody Else. (A Life Guide.)

Real Men Don't Vacuum. And Other Misguided Myths That Cause Conflict in Relationships.

INDEX[3]

A

affirmations, 82, 96
awkward conversations, 4

B

being emotionally whole, 61
being a true friend, 77
best case scenario, 45
building the same future, 25

C

clear vision, 14
confidence, 67, 70, 79
create what you desire, 14

D

dating adventure, 12, 51, 66
dealing with rejection, 47
different values, 25
discomfort with small talk, 79

E

"emotional baggage", 25, 26, 51, 54
"emotional check-in", 5

F

fear of rejection, 47, 80
finding true love, 1, 66, 68, 97
first date fashion tips, 41
fragrance and feelings, 38

G

get(ting) "out there", 28, 34, 47, 66

I

informed decision, 57
insecurity, 50, 79, 80
intense emotional reaction, 50
"it's OK to have preferences", 48

---

[3] The page numbers in this index refer to the printed version of this book.

L

lack confidence, 68
lack of self-worth, 15
letting go of the past, 87
loving, healthy relationship, 4

M

make different choices, 70
manage your feelings, 2
Mr. Right, 15, 34
"must-haves", 23

N

navigate being single, 1
negative self-perception, 16

P

positive anxiety, 37
positive attitude toward online dating, 33
positive frame of mind, 2

R

red flag, 25
"rejection", 2, 4, 47, 50, 51, 54
rejection is not personal, 48
release emotions, 5

release your expectations, 63, 65
replace self-judgement, 70
resolving (release) emotional baggage, 51, 54

S

scream(ing) into the pillow, 10, 52, 80, 81
self-confidence, 70
self-criticism, 6
self-expression exercise, 9
self-judgement, 68, 71, 78
self-worth, 85
sharing a vision of the future, 25
signature scent, 38
slow, unhurried courtship, 59
start dating again, 13, 89, 97

T

take it slow, 56
take your sweet time, 58
"10 free things to do . . .", 30
the dating pool, 29
the dating world, 27
the "point" of a relationship, 22, 24, 25
the world of online dating, 31, 34
true colors, 56, 57

U

unexpected possibilities, 64
unmet emotional needs, 26
unworthy script, 21

V

values, aligned, 57
visualize, 36, 41

W

what are your limitations, 13
write . . . and release, 9
writing exercise, 6, 16, 24, 42, 43, 82

Y

your heart's desire, 13, 14, 16

www.ingramcontent.com/pod-product-compliance
Lightning Source LLC
Chambersburg PA
CBHW030057100526
44591CB00008B/187